Published by OH!
20 Mortimer Street
London W1T 3JW

ISBN 978-1-80069-128-5

Compiled by: David Clayton and Sheahan Arnott
Editorial: Lisa Dyer
Project manager: Russell Porter
Design: Andy Jones
Production: Freencky Portas

A CIP catalogue for this book is available from the British Library

Printed in China

10 9 8 7 6 5 4 3 2 1

THE LITTLE BOOK OF
THE ASHES

THE LITTLE BOOK OF
THE ASHES

THE GREATEST QUOTES &
MOST DEFINING MOMENTS FROM
CRICKET'S OLDEST RIVALRY

CONTENTS

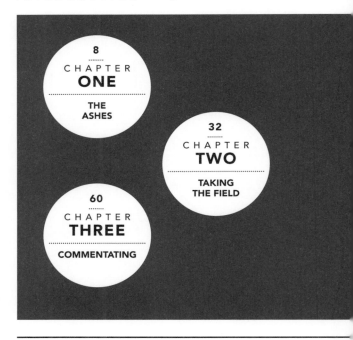

INTRODUCTION

Truly the greatest sporting competition on earth, the Ashes pits two fierce rivals against one another in a battle to the death. OK, maybe not the death, but to a tiny urn full of cricket-bail ashes, certainly.

For centuries before the installation of the Ashes in 1882, England and Australia's kiss-kill-love-hate rivalry erupted often to the surface, as if there was some deep-rooted historical context at the heart of their relationship. All of that, thankfully, was swept aside with the invention of the Ashes annual Test match, giving the two nations a relatively healthy opportunity to prove who's best without the need for name-calling (though, obviously, that does happen). The Ashes were born, and ever since then the two great nations have tried to catch each other out, much to the delight of everyone watching. While

Australia currently leads in total series wins, with no finishing line on the horizon, England, the eternal underdogs, are not out yet.

The Ashes has crowned many legendary cricketing achievements over the decades, many of which are documented in this tiny tome, alongside all the quips and quotes, biffers and dinkers, googlies and grubbers, duck and dollies you could ever dream of. Also included are those unforgettable moments: the perfect centuries; the blink-and-miss-it catches; the whitewashes; the wicket-splitting, as well as a delicious buffet of the most iconic cricketeers ever to wear all-white (you know their names). Yes, this unputdownable pick-me-up proves the Ashes is more than just a game of two sides. It's the ultimate test.

So, sit back and relax and prepare to be bowled over by *The Little Book of the Ashes*, your action-packed assist to the only match that matters.

Chapter 1

The Ashes

The first meeting between the two nations was in 1877 and the series name stems from 1882, when Australia first beat England on English soil.

The following year a small urn containing the ashes of a wicket bail was presented to the captain of the touring English team in Australia and one of sport's greatest rivalries was born…

I swear to you, England will not win this.

Fred "The Demon" Spofforth *to Australian captain Billy Murdoch, after W.G. Grace ran out Sammy Jones in unsportsmanlike fashion. Defending only 85, Spofforth's 7–44 led Australia to the seven-run victory at the Oval, which gave birth to the Ashes in August 1882.*

"

I left six men to get 30 odd runs and they couldn't get them.

"

W.G. Grace, *after England, all out for 77,
failed to get the 85 runs needed to beat Australia. Fast
bowler Fred Spofforth took the last four wickets for only
two runs, leaving England just eight runs short of victory.*

In affectionate remembrance
of
ENGLISH CRICKET,
which died at the Oval
on
29th August 1882.

Deeply lamented by a large circle of sorrowing
friends and acquaintances.

R.I.P.

N.B. – The body will be cremated and the
ashes taken to Australia.

66

We have come to beard the kangaroo
in his den…

99

Ivo Bligh, *the England captain, stokes the flames
ahead of England's tour of Australia, having lost what was
the first test series to be known as "the Ashes".
As reported in the* Melbourne Punch, *February 1883.*

From start to finish, on every sort of wicket, against every sort of bowling, Trumper entranced the eye, inspired his side, demoralized his enemies and made run-getting the easiest thing in the world.

Harry Althem *on the brutal beauty of Victor Trumper in full flight. In 1902 Trumper became the first man to score a century before lunch on Day 1 as Australia won by three runs – the narrowest margin until Edgbaston, 103 years later. Fourth Test, Old Trafford, July 1902.*

"

He cover-drove me to bring up his hundred. The ball was as fast as any I had bowled previously. That glorious stroke has lived in my memory to this day for its ease and perfect timing. I am sure that few among the many thousands present sighted the ball as it raced to the boundary.

"

Harold Larwood *in the foreword to Archie Jackson's biography. The 19-year-old Jackson's 164 on his Test debut in 1929 was his sole Test century, as he passed away aged 23 with only eight Tests to his name. He and Don Bradman were close friends, and many considered Jackson to be the more elegant batsman of the two.*

I've not travelled 6,000 miles to make friends. I'm here to win the Ashes.

Douglas Jardine, *the England skipper tells the Australian press of his intentions ahead of the Bodyline Ashes series, November 1932.*

BODYLINE

The Bodyline series became notorious in cricket circles and proved highly controversial. It was a tactic devised by England on the 1932–33 Ashes tour and was specifically designed to stem the threat of legendary Aussie batsman Don Bradman.

A bodyline delivery was one in which the cricket ball was bowled, at pace, at the body of the batsman, with the idea being that his attempt to defend himself would lead to catching opportunities.

Intimidating and physically threatening, many questioned England's sportsmanship and, such was the fallout, the argument threatened diplomatic relations between the two countries, although this eventually calmed.

If we don't beat you, we'll knock your bloody heads off.

Bill Voce, *the England fast bowler's promise to Australian batsman Vic Richardson before the start of the infamous Bodyline series in Sydney, 2 December 1932. England would win the match by ten wickets.*

66

The feeling is ******* mutual.

99

Douglas Jardine, *responding to teammate Patsy Hendren's comment that "the Australians don't really like you", after a four-hour innings during the Sydney Ashes Test, December 1932.*

Well bowled, Harold!

Douglas Jardine, *making sure the Australians hear his comment after Harold Larwood floors batsman Bill Woodfull with a ball in the chest during the third Test at the Adelaide Oval, January 1933.*

"

Bodyline bowling has assumed such proportions as to menace the best interests of the game, making protection of the body by the batsmen the main consideration. This is causing intensely bitter feeling between the players as well as injury. Unless stopped at once it is likely to upset the friendly relationships existing between Australia and England. **"**

Text of a cable sent to the MCC from the Australian Board of Control for International Cricket during the fifth day of the third Test at Adelaide, 18 January 1933.

I don't want to see you Mr Warner.
There are two teams out there; one is
trying to play cricket and the other
is not. The matter is in your hands,
Mr Warner, and I have nothing further
to say to you. Good afternoon.

Bill Woodfull, *Australia's captain during the infamous
Bodyline series, dismisses England team manager 'Plum'
Warner after the nastiest day's cricket of the series, at the
third Test of the Adelaide Oval, January 1933.*

It were nowt more than a sore throat.

Eddie Paynter, *shrugging off praise after he left his hospital bed to rescue England's first innings with a battling 83. England eventually won the fourth Test in Brisbane by six wickets, February 1933.*

We've got the bastards down there, and we'll keep them there.

Douglas Jardine, *the England captain, attempts to fire up an exhausted Harold Larwood after his plea to be rested for the final Test of the 1932–33 Bodyline series in Sydney. England won the game by eight wickets and the series 4–1, February 1933.*

❝

OK, which of you bastards called Larwood a bastard instead of this bastard?

❞

Vic Richardson, *Australian vice captain, fails to furnish Douglas Jardine with the apology he came to the Australian dressing room looking for. Fifth Test, Sydney, February 1933, as seen on TheGuardian.com, by Rob Smyth, 20 November 2017.*

Oh, forget it, old boy, it's probably cost us the rubber, but what the hell!

Gubby Allen, *the England captain, tries to console R.W.V. Robins when, in the second innings of the third Test, in January 1937, he dropped Don Bradman at 24 – who went on to score a magnificent 270 on the way to an Australia victory!*

If I could play an innings like that,
I would be a very proud man, Stan.

Don Bradman *to Stan McCabe after the
latter's boundary-laden 232 during the first Test, June
1938. McCabe scored 127 runs in a session during his
innings – still an Ashes record to this day.*

THE INVINCIBLES

The only Test match side to play an entire tour of England without losing a match was the 1948 "Invincibles" led by Don Bradman.

The team won 25 of their 34 matches – 17 of them by an innings – and drew the other 9. They made less than 200 only twice on the tour, yet bowled their opposition out under 200 37 times. Eleven batsmen made centuries, and seven passed 1,000 runs on the tour.

THE PLAYERS:

Don Bradman (captain), Lindsay Hassett (vice captain), Arthur Morris, Sid Barnes, Bill Brown, Ron Hamence, Neil Harvey, Ian Johnson, Bill Johnston, Ray Lindwall, Sam Loxton, Colin McCool, Keith Miller, Doug Ring, Ron Saggers, Don Tallon and Ernie Toshack.

66

Most of his cricket was played at the highest level, on the best wickets and against strong opposition. His skill, unaccompanied by histrionics, was something for the connoisseur to savour.

99

A cricket writer in England summarizing Ray Lindwall's contribution to the Invincibles tour. Lindwall would end up with 27 Test wickets despite carrying an injury at the start of the tour. In the final Test at the Oval, Don Bradman would describe Lindwall's spell after lunch on the first day, in which he took five wickets for eight runs in 8.1 overs, as "the most devastating and one of the fastest I ever saw in Test cricket", August 1948.

One of the most volatile cricketers of any age. Long, rangy, athletic type – drove the ball with tremendous power... Dangerous bowler with the new ball, swinging it both ways not much short of [Ray] Lindwalls speed... In 1948 he was the best slip field in the world. Altogether, a crowd-pleasing personality.

Don Bradman, *full of praise for Kieth Miller, who would go on to retire in 1956 with the best statistics of any all-rounder at the time.*

'Australianism' means single-minded determination to win – to win within the laws but, if necessary, to the last limit within them.

John Arlott, *writing in 1949, reflecting on the winning mentality of Australian cricketers a year after Don Bradman's Invicibles tour of England.*

Chapter 2

Taking the Field

In more recent times, cricket has been transformed by innovative new formats and technological changes, but the Ashes rivalry has never ceased to deliver extraordinary stories.

As new generations of players evolve, there is no lacking in their desire to take to the field, to represent their country and to crush the opposition.

66

No beggar got all 10 when I was
bowling at the other end.

99

Sydney Barnes, *one of England's greatest bowlers,
who held the record for the most number of wickets in a
Test innings (9 for 103) for 42 years, commenting after
spin bowler Jim Laker had taken all ten Australian wickets
at Old Trafford, Manchester, on 31 July 1956.*

"

It was not with batting supremacy nor bowling superiority that Australia eclipsed us. It was intestinal fortitude, or to put it briefly still: guts… As for Burge, he was Australia himself.

"

Denzil Batchelor *was in awe of Peter Burge's rear-guard 160, which won Australia the Test, and the series, and earned him the moniker the "Lion of Leeds", at the third Test at Headingley, July 1964.*

Faster and straighter, right?

Bob Willis, *checking with skipper Mike Brearley ahead of an explosive spell of second-innings bowling at Headingley that earned him figures of 8–43 and helped England to a famous win, 21 July 1981.*

❝

Tell Bob to bowl straight at Dennis,
it doesn't matter what length.

❞

Mike Gatting, *with England desperate to get the*
final Australian wicket at Headingley, advises skipper Mike
Brearley on a method of dismissing Dennis Lillee – the
next delivery, Willis followed the instructions and Gatting
caught Lillee's late attempt at a drive to win the third Test
by 18 runs and level the series at 1–1, 21 July 1981.

Growing up, my education about Test cricket came from dad's video of the 1981 Ashes series – and Ian Botham's incredible match at Headingley.

James Anderson, *England's record wicket-taker, on his early education, as quoted in his column in* The Sun, *31 July 2018.*

"
I suppose me mum'll speak to me.
Reckon me dad will too. And my wife.
But who else?
"

Kim Hughes, *Australian captain, after losing,
having made England follow-on, at the third Test
at Headingley, 1981.*

Hobbs, Hammond and Broad – it
doesn't quite ring true, does it?

Chris Broad, *after scoring a third successive Ashes Test
century in Melbourne and consigning Australia to their
14th consecutive Test without a victory, marking an historic
low, January 1986.*

"

Imagine Boonie sat at the table when someone comes along and knocks his VB off the side. He moved so quickly to his right to get a hand under the ball, it was as if he was determined not only to catch his beer but not to spill a drop either.

"

Ian Botham *was in awe of David Boon's diving bat-pad catch to dismiss Devon Malcolm and give Shane Warne a Test hat-trick at the second Test at the Melbourne Cricket Ground (MCG), 29 December 1994.*

THE 2005 ASHES

The 2005 Ashes series remains one of the most celebrated in English cricket history, the BBC reporting it as "the most thrilling series ever".

After 18 years of series losses against the Aussies, and Australia confident of another series win, England fought hard in the five-match battle, eventually winning 2–1, having been convincingly beaten in the first Test. England won the second Test by two runs, the smallest margin in Ashes test history, and then in the fourth Test forced Australia to follow-on, the first time in 191 Tests.

Suffice to say, the victory produced an outpouring of joy among English cricket fans.

"

This is absolutely sensational. I was speechless when it all happened yesterday and I'm virtually speechless again today. I'm taking it all in and, I've got to say, this is great for the game of cricket.

"

Kevin Pietersen, *still trying to let it all sink in after winning the Ashes for the first time in 18 years, September 2005.*

"

We've done a lot in the last two years but I didn't think we were quite ready to do what we have done in this series. I'm over the moon. To appear in an Ashes series and to win it is difficult to put into words. Only when we all head home will we finally get a chance to realize what we've achieved. **"**

Marcus Trescothick, *scorer of 431 runs in the 2005 Ashes series, reflects on a job very well done, 13 September 2005.*

"

It was a mixture of bad bowling, good shots and arse.

"

Jason Gillespie *on his own performance in the 2005 series, as quoted in the* Sydney Morning Herald, October 2005.

I'm struggling now, I've not been to bed yet and behind these sunglasses is a thousand stories.

Andrew "Freddie" Flintoff, *still struggling the day after England reclaimed the Ashes in style at the Oval, 13 September 2005.*

I don't care if Tony Blair or Robbie Williams bowl to me the first ball of the Ashes series. All my teammates and I care about is winning back the Ashes.

Justin Langer *before the start of the 2006–07 series. Perhaps Tony or Robbie might have made a better fist of it than Steve Harmison?*

I brought Monty Panesar on and he hit him for six into the stands over mid-on, so I put mid-on back thinking 'he won't do that again'. So he hit it further. And he hit it further again, and further again. The field was scattered everywhere, but I didn't have enough fielders.

Andrew "Freddie" Flintoff, *on trying to contain a rampant Adam Gilchrist on his way to the then second-fastest hundred in Test history. Flintoff had tormented Gilchrist throughout the previous seven tests between the two countries, and Gilly's home-ground onslaught was sweet revenge for the sleepless nights he'd given him. At the third Test at the Western Australian Cricket Association (WACA), December 2006.*

"

To win 5–0 is a fantastic achievement by this group of guys. The team's played some sensational cricket through the whole summer. England have payed some good cricket at times too, but when the big moments came the Australian team stood up.

"

Shane Warne, *praising a wonderful team effort after securing a whitewash 5–0 victory over England. This last match of the series would the last Test game for Warne, along with Glenn McGrath and Justin Langer, who all retired. Sydney, 6 January 2007.*

66

I was actually hoping to get a chance to bat with Justin today and I was a bit filthy with Matty (Hayden) for not getting out.

99

Ricky Ponting, *Australia's captain, getting emotional as he admitted the retirements of Warne, McGrath and Langer at the end of the series had got to him. Sydney, 6 January 2007.*

"

Trent Bridge, 2013, is my favourite Test. An Ashes opener and England won a thriller by 14 runs. I managed to take ten wickets, which helps. **"**

James Anderson, *his modesty getting the better of him! England would go on to win the summer series 3–0, and then travel to Australia for a back-to-back series just a few months later.*

It's pathetic – there is no other word. It's humilitation. England have disintegrated. How do you get bowled out in 32 overs? It's bad enough to lose all five, but it's how you lose.

Geoffrey Boycott, *leaving little to the imagination on what his thoughts were on the only third 5–0 whitewash in Ashes history, and just five months after England had beaten an Australian team branded "the worst team ever to tour England". Sydney, 7 January 2014.*

66

When you're on top of your game like that it feels bloody good. It feels like you're floating. In your run-up, you know what ball you want to bowl, where you want to bowl it. You don't feel like you can bowl a bad ball, or do anything wrong. It's what you play the game for.

99

Mitchell Johnson, *describiing what it's like to be in the best form of your life. His 37 wickets at an average of 13.9 were not just the reason Australia won back the ashes, he dismantled England and ended careers. January 2014.*

60 all out??? What!!!
Booooooooooooom!!!

Kevin Pietersen, *in a tweet after the Aussies are skittled for 60 in the fourth Test at Trent Bridge, Nottingham, 6 August 2015.*

❝

It was an amazing feeling, especially
being at Trent Bridge, somewhere
where I have got such great
connection. It was a bit of a daze up
until Joe Root walked off at the end of
the day when it was game done. **❞**

Stuart Broad, *reflecting on his amazing 8 for 15
bowling figures as the Aussies fell to 60 all out. Australia's
extras (14) were higher than any of their batsmen, the first
time extras had out-scored a teams top-scoring batsman
in Ashes history.*

We've done something I didn't think was quite possible at the beginning of the summer.

Alastair Cook, *on how England had grown during the 2015 series, after regaining the Ashes on the third day of the fourth Test at Trent Bridge, 8 August 2015.*

"

I would like a better record here in Australia.

"

James Anderson, *despite a poor England performance in the 2017–18 series in Australia, would end the tour as England's fourth-best wicket-taker. Now, with more than 600 Test wickets to his name, Anderson is the leading wicket taker of all time in Test cricket.*

He's a bit of a freak to be able to, time and time again, produce match-winning performances like that.

Joe Root, *the England captain's "affectionate" description of Ben Stokes' Ashes heroics at Headingley. His vice captain had guided England to that astonishing third Test Ashes win, with his superb 135 not out, after England were bowled out for 67 in the first innings and set 359 to win at the start of the second innings, on 25 August 2019.*

"

When a number 11 comes out needing 70 to win, I knew what I had to do in terms of the game situation. The only time I started to get a little bit nervous or panicking was when we got into single figures.

"

Ben Stokes *recalling his nervy final stand with Jack Leach the day after England level the 2019 Ashes series at Headingley, 26 August 2019.*

Chapter 3

Commentating

Ever since cricket was first broadcast, the wit, wisdom and wickedness of commentators have often been as iconic as the matches themselves.

They are a unique breed – informed, opinionated and insightful, often having to talk for hours about God's Own Game ... and here are some of their best thoughts, observations and missives.

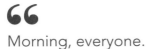

Morning, everyone.

Richie Benaud *gets us off on another*
"marvellous" day of Ashes cricket commentary.

"

A team of five or six decoders would put
the cables into readable form from which
the commentators would operate…
The sound of the bat striking the ball
was generated by a pencil in the hands
of the commentator tapping on a round
piece of wood on the desk, the harder
the stroke seemed on the cable, the more
resounding the tap of the pencil! **"**

Alan McGilvray *on how they broadcast cricket from
the other side of the world in the early days of the ABC.
McGilvray and his team mastered the art of turning a 25-word
telegram into flowing descriptions of Bradman's brilliance.*

There's Neil Harvey standing at leg slip with his legs wide apart, waiting for a tickle.

Brian Johnston *in classic form ... 1961.*

"

Don't bother looking for that, let alone chasing it. That's gone straight into the confectionary stall and out again.

"

Richie Benaud, *commentating after one of Ian Botham's huge slog shots in his match-winning innings at Headingley during the third Test, July 1981.*

A fart competing with thunder.

Graham Gooch, *making a brutally honest appraisal of England's fortunes in the 1990–91 Ashes series, which Australia won 3–0, February 1991.*

England trained and grass grew at the MCG yesterday, two activities virtually indistinguishable from each other in tempo.

Greg Baum, *the Australian journalist, was unimpressed with the tourists' intensity at the second Test at the MCG, 1994–95.*

Jonathan Agnew: But he could come back tomorrow? He could come back, have good old Harmison – a bit of a loosener on the leg stump and pick it off for two...

Kerry O'Keefe: Stuff the silver – we come for the gold!

Poms would come back tomorrow – Aussies want it now!

We're instant people. COME ON STEPHEN!

Jonathan Agnew: 233 for 5.

Dawson comes up and bowls to Waugh, who drives – AND DRIVES THROUGH THE OFF-SIDE FOR HIS HUNDRED!

That is extraordinary.

And Steve Waugh, a man of little emotion, can barely restrain himself now.

Jonathan Agnew and **Kerry O'Keefe** *in contrast as Steve Waugh's last ball century against the Old Enemy stopped the nation. Fifth Test, 2002–03.*

One day we'll lose the Ashes, and it will be as horrific as waking up after a night on the drink in a room full of images of Camilla Parker Bowles.

Sydney-based newspaper the Daily Telegraph *before the 2005 series. Unfortunately, Australia did lose, but it wasn't quite as bad as a hangover surrounded by pictures of the Duchess of Cornwall. Still pretty bad though. As seen on ESPNcricinfo.com, Cricinfo staff, 12 September 2005.*

I definitely believe if any of our batsmen get out to Giles in the Tests they should go and hang themselves. But I'm confident that won't happen.

Terry Alderman *knows a thing or two about taking wickets in the Ashes, but Giles had the last laugh in England's famous 2005 series win.*

He likes the English so much he changed the series for them with the most stupid decision he'll ever make in his life.

Sir Geoffrey Boycott, *on Aussie captain Ricky Ponting's decision to bowl at the crucial Edgbaston Ashes Test, 4 August 2005.*

"

This has been the most exhilarating, entertaining, tension-packed series there has ever been. It's a big statement to make but, let's be honest, we're talking about modern cricket here in the modern era — nothing matches this in any way. To witness and experience this has been a dream.

"

Jonathan Agnew, *as Aggers doing what Aggers does best, summing up the unforgettable summer of 2005 on BBC Radio 5 Live, September 2005.*

The first ball of the first test match…
Whooooah wide delivery taken at slip
by the skipper. The nerves are showing
already!

Bill Lawry was as shocked as anyone when Steve
Harmison's first ball of the most-anticipated Ashes series
in history flew straight to second slip. If Harmison's fiery
spell at Lord's a year early set the tone for the 2005 series,
then his wayward loosener did the same for Australia's
5–0 whitewash. First Test, at the "Gabba", 2006–07.

66

There are two ways to play Warne, and somewhere between their two innings England decided to abandon the Fred Astaire routine, which had served them so well for the first two days, and switch to the kind of footwork that would have embarrassed a boxful of battery hens.

99

Martin Johnson, *on the English collapse that led to "Amazing Adelaide" in the 2006–07 series. Second Test at the Adelaide Oval, December 2006.*

Adelaide '06 deserves to haunt this
generation of English cricketers
as Headingley '81 once haunted
Australians.

Gideon Haigh, *on England's own "losing the
un-loseable Test". Second Test at the Adelaide Oval,
December 2006.*

❝

It's one hell of a beating, isn't it? I mean, they have just been murdered?

❞

Sir Geoffrey Boycott *gives an uncompromising appraisal of England's 2007 Ashes performance after a 5–0 defeat, only the second time an Ashes series had been won by that margin, on Sky Sports, January 2007.*

I think England will win a Test.
My concern is Australia will probably
win two.

Sir Geoffrey Boycott, *ever the pessimist! Despite Australia winning the first Test, England would go on to win the series 2–1, with Flintoff becoming the first Englishman to take over 20 wickets and score over 400 runs in a Test series, in June 2009.*

"

Oh well bowled, that's close... he's given him! He's given him!
Peter Siddle's got a hat-trick on his birthday!

"

Mark Taylor *couldn't contain his excitement when Australia's vegan fast bowler trapped Stuart Broad in front to claim the first Ashes hat-trick since 1994 during the first Test at the "Gabba", 25 November 2010.*

The way things are going, the next Ashes series cannot come too quickly for England. What a shame that we have to wait until 2013 to play this lot again.

Sir Geoffrey Boycott, *talking on Sky Sports as England wrap up a 3–1 series win in the 2011 Ashes at Sydney, January 2011.*

Each time they set a trap for him and he falls for it. He is a mug and the Aussies are laughing. They think he is a sucker.

Sir Geoffrey Boycott, *on Kevin Pietersen's "Achilles Heel" dismissals during the Ashes whitewash Down Under. As reported in the* Daily Telegraph, *December 2013.*

Just 599 days after handing over the urn, Cook has his redemption.

Nasser Hussain, *commentating on Sky Sports as England regain the Ashes by going 3–1 up at Trent Bridge, July 2015.*

"

Cut away. Cut away for four!
What an innings. What a player.
Take a bow, Ben Stokes. The Ashes
are well and truly alive because of
one cricketer.

"

Nasser Hussain, *commentating on Sky Sports as
Ben Stokes scores the winning runs in the third Ashes Test
at Headingley, 25 August 2019.*

Quite how Ben had the strength to play an innings like that after his World Cup heroics and subsequent Tests was something else. Naturally, his unbeaten 135 will be compared to Ian Botham's 149 at Headingley 38 years ago – and let me tell you that Ben's is the better knock.

Bob Willis, *comparing Ben Stokes heroics in the third Test at Headingley to Ian Botham's in 1981, 25 August 2019.*

66

And that's what it is as far as I'm concerned – time to say goodbye. I can add to that: thank you for having me. It's been absolutely marvellous for 42 years. I've loved every moment of it. And it's been a privilege to go into everyone's living room throughout that time. What's even better – it's been a great deal of fun. [McGrath bowls Pietersen] But not so for the batsman.

99

Richie Benaud *bids his farewell to English audiences as the 2005 series comes to an end. But a pro until the last – Richie doesn't let the cricket get in the way of his goodbye. Fifth Test at the Oval, 12 September 2005.*

Chapter 4

Sledging

Intimidation, if done well, is an art. And sledging is intimidation at its finest.

Ranging from the comical to the outright insulting, sledging's single aim is to unsettle the opposition in order to distract them and disturb their concentration.

Some get hooked in, others love the "banter", while those with more fragile egos wither in front of our eyes.

The chief offender was Warwick Armstrong, who got very nasty and unsportsmanlike.

Jack Hobbs, *unimpressed by Aussie all-rounder Armstrong's sledging after the Headingley Test match, which the tourists won to go 2–1 up in the series, July 1909.*

"

Oi, leave our flies alone, Jardine –
they're the only flamin' friends you've
got here!

"

*Sledging is not always limited to the 22 on-field
combatants, as Douglas Jardine discovered during this
run-in with legendary heckler "Yabba". Fifth Test at the
Sydney Cricket Ground (SCG), December 1932.*

Bailey, I wish you were a statue and I was a pigeon.

Trevor "Barnacle" Bailey, *England's all-rounder whose stubborn defensive style of play earned him his nickname, draws the ire of the crowd during yet another yawn-inducing innings. Fifth Test at the MCG, January 1955.*

66

Well, Fred, I am on 468 runs for the series, so I'd like my 500th. And, anyway, you're a good enough bowler to get me out without me having to give it to you. Now piss off.

99

Colin McDonald – *sharp-tongued and stout in defence – after Fred Trueman told him that he'd taken 99 Test wickets to that point. But McDonald got his 500th run shortly after, and Trueman had to wait until his next test to get to 100 wickets. Fifth Test at the MCG, February 1959.*

I have always believed sledging to
be both immature and stupid and
it surprises me that international
cricketers can be affected by it.
It has always formed more of a part of
the Australian game than the English
game. I remember our tour of Australia
in 1970–71 – the Chappell brothers,
Ian and Greg, were never backward
in coming forward and Dennis Lillee
would motivate himself by geeing up
the opposition.

But the levels of verbal abuse then were nothing like they are now. To me it seems a waste of breath and energy.

Bob Willis, *England's legendary fast bowler, gives his views on sledging in an impassioned article in the* Evening Standard. *Bob was not one for mind games... 3 July 2015.*

Just remember who started this: those bastards. But we'll finish it.

Dennis Lillee *to his teammates after being bounced by England captain Tony Greig. Between this incident and "I intend to make them grovel", surely no cricketer had a worse record of poking the bear than Greig. At the MCC in Australia, December 1974.*

"
Yeah, I'd drink with 'em. Trouble is, ya can never find any Poms to drink with, eh Dennis?

"

Jeff Thomson *discovers that, when you're sending a steady stream of Englishmen to the hospital, it's hard to find one who wants to share a pint. December 1974.*

Take a good look at this arse of mine,
you'll see plenty of it this summer.

David Steele, *after the England batsman arrives at the crease in the second Test at Lord's and offers some solid advice to Australian keeper Rod Marsh, 31 July 1975.*

"
You've got some shit on the end of
your bat… [Batsman looks at the toe].
Wrong end, mate.
"

Dennis Lillee *with one of his favourites, and one
he's reported to have levelled at multiple batsmen
throughout his career.*

It's no good hitting me there, mate, there's nothing to damage.

Derek Randall, *after surviving a Dennis Lillee bouncer, despite the ball hitting his head on the fourth day of the Centenary Test at the MCG, 17 March 1977.*

"

Playing against a team with Ian Chappell as captain turns a cricket match into gang warfare.

"

Mike Brearley, *on his hard-edged, win-at-all-costs Australian counterpart.*

Chappell was a coward. He needed a crowd around him before he would say anything. He was sour like milk that had been sitting in the sun for a week.

Ian Botham *sharing a frank opinion on Aussie legend Ian Chappell in Melbourne, 1977 – it was a feud that lasted for years and is reported to have ended at least once in fisticuffs. As seen on Sportskeeda.com, Tanya Rudra, 16 November 2017.*

" You have done for Australian cricket what the Boston Strangler did for door-to-door salesmen. **"**

Jack Birney, *Australian politician, in a note to Geoffrey Boycott after the dour Yorkshireman batted all day for 63*. Second Test at the WACA, December 1978.*

I know you think I'm great Hoggy, but no need to get down on your knees.

Ian Botham, *serving a classic Beefy line to Aussie fast bowler Rod Hogg, who could have chosen a better place to lose his balance… July 1981.*

66

Rod Marsh: "How's your wife and my kids?"

Ian Botham: "The wife's fine, but the kids are retarded."

99

Ian Botham, *England all-rounder, delivers a quick comeback to Rod Marsh as he arrives at the crease – believed to be at the "Gabba" in Brisbane for the first Test, November 1986.*

Merv Hughes: "You can't f***ing bat."

Robin Smith strikes the next ball to the boundary for four and responds.

Robin Smith: "Hey Merv, we make a fine pair. I can't f***ing bat and you can't f***ing bowl."

Words exchanged during the second Test at Lord's – a game Australia go on to win by six wickets, June 1989.

66

Didn't you go to the team meeting?
They would have told you you can't
bowl on middle-and-leg to me. **99**

Dean Jones *to Angus Fraser after whipping him
through midwicket for four at Trent Bridge, August 1989.*

Would you like me to bowl a piano
and see if you can play that?

Merv Hughes *to Graham Gooch after playing
and missing a number of consecutive deliveries.*

“

What do you think this is, a f***ing tea party? No you can't have a f***ing glass of water. You can f***ing wait like all the rest of us.

”

Allan Border – *nicknamed "Captain Grumpy" for a reason – was not about to let Robin Smith quench his thirst at the fifth Test at Trent Bridge, August 1989.*

Ian Healy: "You're a f****** cheat."

Mike Atherton: "When in Rome, dear boy."

Mike Atherton, *England skipper, delivers a classy riposte to wicketkeeper Ian Healy after being given not-out despite edging the ball as England battled to save the third Test in Sydney, January 1991.*

66

If you turn the bat over you'll get the instructions mate.

99

Merv Hughes *to Robin Smith after another play-and-miss. First Test at Old Trafford, June 1993.*

I'm not talking to anyone in the British media. They are all pricks.

Allan Border, *after winning back the Ashes in 1989. Border returned to England in 1993 as jovial and warm as ever. Australia in England, 1993.*

66

Waugh! Ooh! What is he good for?
Absolutely nothing!

99

*England fans serenade the Aussie batsman to the tune of
Edwin Starr's "War" during the 1993 Ashes third Test at
Headingley. Waugh went on to score 157 not out.*

"

You're sh*t Hayden – and so is your chicken casserole!

"

Australia's Matthew Hayden is taunted by an England fan as he walks out in the first Test at Old Trafford – and the casserole pun? He'd released a cookery book earlier that year… 3 June 1993.

"

If you turn the bat over there's instructions on the back.

"

Merve Hughes, *Aussie fast bowler, to Graeme Hick after he'd played and missed another shot during the first Test at Old Trafford, 4 June 1993.*

Tufnell! Can I borrow your brain? I'm building an idiot.

99

Ian Healey, *Aussie wicketkeeper, to the England spinner Phil Tufnell during the 1994–95 Ashes series at the "Gabba", 24 November 1994.*

66

If you're playing against the
Australians, you don't walk.

99

Ian Botham, *giving advice for any England cricketer
facing the Aussies. As stated in court during Imran Khan's
libel action case, 1996.*

That could be anywhere inside a three-mile radius.

Ian Healy, *the gold standard for mouthy wicketkeepers, didn't miss out when Steve Waugh told Ricky Ponting to field under Nasser Hussain's nose.*

"

Mark Waugh: F*** me, look who it is? Mate, what are you doing out here, there's no way you're good enough to play for England.

James Ormond: Maybe not, but at least I'm the best player in my family.

"

James Ormond, *as England debutant responding to Mark Waugh's unsubtle sledging by suggesting brother Steve Waugh was the superior of the siblings, August 2001.*

All the palaver caused me to burn my toast!

Duncan Fletcher, *England coach, makes light of the aftermath of the controversial Ricky Ponting run out in Trent Bridge by a sub fielder (Gary Pratt) – much to Ponting's chagrin, which he made clear to Fletcher as he returned to the dressing room, August 2005.*

66

Aussie sledging? I'm just glad they've heard of me!

99

Monty Panesar, *England's left-arm spinner, prior to the 2006–07 Ashes series, after hearing that the Australian players would take an aggressive approach towards him.*

I have prepared for the worst-case scenario, but it could be even worse than that.

Monty Panesar, *ready to face the vociferous crowds in Australia before the 2006–07 tour, unaware that England would collapse to a 5–0 defeat, the first whitewash in an Ashes series since 1920–21.*

66

How can you have a clash of cultures when you're playing against a country with no culture?

99

David Gower, *posing a provocative question on Sky Sport ahead of England's Ashes series Down Under. As quoted in the* Radio Times, *July 2013.*

I definitely think they're rattled by it. They don't like it at all. Their coach has come out and wanted a truce from what I've heard, but that's not going to change from our end.

Mitchell Johnson, *on Australia's intimidatory tactics. England in Australia, 2013–14.*

"

Get ready for a broken f***ing arm!

"

Michael Clarke *tries to hurry up Jimmy Anderson after the latter was more interested in exchanging words with George Bailey than facing a fired-up Mitchell Johnson. First Test at the "Gabba", December 2013.*

Dealing with sledging is an individual thing. For me, I am not going to take abuse from David Warner or anyone else and not have a word back. But it is down to the person.

James Anderson, *giving as good as he gets, as reported in* The Guardian, *21 January 2015.*

"

I am looking forward to the Ashes.
I had been predicting 5–0, but now I
have changed my prediction. I am now
predicting 10–0 because Australia is
already up 5–0 from the last tour.

"

Glenn McGrath *confidently tipping Australia for
back-to-back whitewash victories prior to the 2015 series.
Unfortunately, England's response was a 3–2 series win.
June 2015.*

It's the sort of score you expect to see at the Under-9s on the village green.

Ian Botham *speaking on Sky Sports, on Australia's pitiful 60 all out against England in the fourth Test at Trent Bridge. An explosive spell of bowling by Stuart Broad skittles the Aussies out as the fast bowler takes 8 for 15… 6 August 2015.*

"

The other advantage England have when Tufnell is bowling is that he isn't fielding.

"

Ian Chappell *was never one to mince his words, whether on the field or behind the mic. As seen on* FoxSports.com.au, *31 October 2017.*

Chapter 5

Ashes Legends

Cricket is full of legends, from the great batsmen and bowlers, to the thrilling all-rounders and master tacticians.

W.G. Grace to Donald Bradman; Geoff Boycott to Ricky Ponting; Ian Botham to Shane Warne – the great and the good are recognized in this chapter with their words of wisdom...

He had no style, and yet he was all style. He had three strokes for every ball.

C.B. Fry, *on Victor Trumper. Trumper was such a revered figure that for a long time people were hesitant to compare Bradman to the turn-of-the-century legend.*

66

I honestly think that Australia have got to thank one man – one man only for their success. That man is Warwick Armstrong, probably one of the best captains ever sent to England from Australia.

99

Frank Foster, *the England all-rounder who had to retire from cricket after an injury in 1915, was still in awe of the Big Ship's ability to lead his team. Armstrong captained his country ten times – all against England – for eight wins and two draws.*

If ever there was a man singled out as a king of sport it was Mr Armstrong, who had gone out to give the people of England a chance to regain the Ashes and who had returned, like Imperial Caesar, who came, saw and conquered.

Billy Hughes, the Australian Prime Minister, welcomes home Warwick "Big Ship" Armstrong, following Australia's 3–0 series. Australia lost just two of their 38 matches on the tour. Australia in England, 1921.

66

Test cricket is not a light-hearted
business, especially that between
England and Australia.

99

Don Bradman *– no one has ever been more serious
about making runs against England.*

DON BRADMAN

Sir Donald "the Don" Bradman was, beyond any doubt, the greatest batsman of the 20th century.

He was only 20 when he made his test debut in the first Test in the 1928–29 Ashes series. Although Test match opponents were fewer and further between in his day, no one felt the brunt of Don Bradman's quick blade more than England.

Bradman remains the only player to score 5,000 Test match runs against one opponent, holds the record for most runs in an Ashes series (974 runs at 139.14 in 1930) and is the only player to score a test triple century in a day – 309* at Leeds in 1930.

He captained the "Invincibles" team in 1948 and retired from Test cricket at the end of that series tour.

"

When you play Test cricket you don't give Englishmen an inch. Play it tough, all the way. Grind them into the dust.

"

Don Bradman *didn't grind the Old Enemy down mentally like some of those who followed; he did it with bladesmanship and an unmatched appetite for runs.*

Bodyline was devised to stifle Bradman's batting genius. They said I was a killer with the ball, without taking into account that Bradman, with the bat, was the greatest killer of all.

Harold Larwood, *on the man he was charged to stop at all costs.*

"

Don Bradman will bat no more against England, and two contrary feelings dispute within us: relief, that our bowlers will no longer be oppressed by this phenomenon; regret, that a miracle has been removed from among us. So must ancient Italy have felt when she heard of the death of Hannibal.

"

R.C. Robertson-Glasgow, *in reverent awe upon Bradman's retirement. Only Shane Warne has shown a mastery over an opponent worth mentioning in the same breath in the years since "the Don" laid down his bat.*

Oh, for a word of rare Cardusean fire
Oh, for a song upon the poet's lyre
Oh, that the bells should ring a
    noble peal
To hymn the glories of our
    sinister Neil.

Sir Robert Menzies, *Australian Prime Minister, was an unabashed cricket tragic. Menzies hosted a dinner for the Australian team in London during their 1953 tour, and "entertained" the guests with self-penned poems about his cricketing idols – such as this one about stylish left-hander Neil Harvey. "Cardusean" references Neville Cardus, the legendary cricket journalist. Australia in England, 1953.*

66

Ashes to Ashes, dust to dust, if
Thomson don't get ya, Lillee must.

99

*A caption in the Sydney Daily Telegraph summed up
England's experience in Australia during their 1974–75
tour, at the MCC in Australia, February 1975.*

He is so dedicated to the perfection
of his own batting technique that he is
sometimes oblivious to the feelings and
aspirations of his teammates.

Arthur Connell, *chairman of the Yorkshire committee,
on Sir Geoffrey Boycott in 1978.*

"

Geoffrey Boycott is the only fellow I've met who fell in love with himself at a young age and has remained faithful ever since.

"

Dennis Lillee *didn't have much respect for any batsman, least of all the dour English opener. As seen on FoxSports.com.au, October 31, 2017.*

Lillee and Thomson remain a combination to conjure with, as sinister in England as Burke and Hare, or Bismarck and Tirpitz.

Gideon Haigh, *writer and journalist, on the two names that struck fear in the hearts of English batsmen like no one else, until Mitchell Johnson almost 40 years later.*

BOTHAM'S ASHES

Sir Ian Botham, OBE, is regarded as one of the greatest all-rounders the world has ever seen.

He was the one-time leading wicket-taker in international cricket but is perhaps best known for his incredible performance in the 1981 Ashes Test against Australia where his unbeaten 149 steered England to a win that had been – at one stage – a 500 to 1 chance.

His career stats of 102 Tests, 5,200 runs and 383 wickets underlines his legendary status among England fans – and boy, did he love winding the Aussies up!

66

He didn't want to bowl, you know…

99

Mike Brearley, *the England skipper, reveals his matchwinner Ian Botham hadn't wanted to bowl ahead of Beefy's finest hour for England – and what later would become known as "Botham's Ashes", 21 July 1981.*

❝

You don't fancy hanging around
on this wicket for a day and a half,
do you? Right. Come on, let's give
it some humpty.

❞

Ian Botham, *telling Graham Dilley, with England
struggling badly, that it's time to take the game to the
Aussies at Headingley. He will go on to score an unbeaten
149 as England – at one stage quoted as high as 500 to 1
to win – recover to win by 18 runs, July 1981.*

He came into the match having lost the captaincy after a pair at Lord's and when he came to the crease in the second innings as England followed on, the situation was hopeless. Only nobody had told Beefy.

Australia's Daily Telegraph *newspaper reporting on Ian Botham's second innings unbeaten 149 that created history by helping England become only the second side to win after being forced to follow on. At Headingley, July 1981.*

66

A Test match without Botham is like a
horror film without Boris Karloff.

99

Fred Truman, *the Yorkshireman's forthright view of an
England side bereft of Beefy, circa 1989.*

... He still doesn't know!

99

Richie Benaud, *as understated as ever, in awe of Shane Warne's "ball of the century", just as the rest of us. First Test at Old Trafford, June 1993.*

66

How anyone can spin a ball the width of Gatting boggles the mind.

99

Martin Johnson, *writing in the* Independent, *on Shane Warne's "ball of the century", which bowled out Mike Gatting on Day 2 of the first Test at Old Trafford, 4 June 1993.*

I suppose I can say I was there at the moment he first indicated his potential to the wider world. There or thereabouts anyway.

Mike Gatting, *on simply being there (or thereabouts) with Shane Warne from the beginning.*

"

My tactic would be to take a
quick single and observe him from
the other end.

"

Geoffrey Boycott, *the Sky Sports commentator,
reveals how he would have faced Shane Warne in
February 1994.*

There it is! Wicket number 700! And they can't catch him. Shane Warne – through the gate – has got Strauss.

Mark Taylor *celebrates with the 89,000 other fans there to see Shane Warne become the first man to take 700 Test wickets. Warne's 700th was also his 50th wicket at his home ground, and the first in his 37th, and final, Test match five-wicket haul. During the third Test at the MCG, December 2006.*

"

England have no McGrath-ish bowlers, there are hardly any McGrath-ish bowlers – except for McGrath.

"

Stuart Law *correctly pointing out that Australia's metronomic fast bowler was in a class of one.*

That Glenn McGrath: what a bastard.

Mick Jagger *on one of England's chief Ashes tormentors.*

Get a single down the other end and watch someone else play him.

Geoffrey Boycott, *giving nothing if not consistent advice on how he'd handle facing Glenn McGrath.*

The best batsman I had the privilege to play against.

Michael Vaughan *on Ricky Ponting.*

66

I just try to bore the batsmen out.
There's no secret, really. I've always
said that you can land 99 balls out of
100 where you want them, just hitting
the top off-stump, then you will take
wickets. It's pretty simple stuff, but the
complicated thing is to keep it simple.
That's what I've done reasonably well
through my career.

99

Glen McGrath *in 2005 at Lord's after becoming the
fourth player and first seamer to reach 500 Test wickets.*

Chapter 6

Extras

Like all good innings, extra's will always add a few unexpected additions to the final score.

In this final chapter we take a closer look at the more curious and funnier side of Ashes cricket – from the extraordinary-but-true stories and unbelievable moments, to amazing facts that defied the odds and scenes that you'll find hard to believe.

This is the other side of the Ashes. Take it away...

"

The sound of his bat somehow puts
me in mind of vintage port...

"

A.A. Milne, *the Winnie-the-Pooh creator, describes
another glorious Ashes innings by Jack "The Master"
Hobbs on his final Ashes tour, 1928.*

“

Australians will always fight for those 22 yards. Lord's and its traditions belong to Australia just as much as England.

”

John Curtin, *Australian Prime Minister, was talking as much about winning Test matches as he was winning wars when he said this in a speech at Lord's in 1944.*

Like an old lady poking with her umbrella at a wasp's nest.

John Arlott, *BBC* Test Match Special's *long-time commentator on the unique batting style of Australia's Ernie Toshack, back in 1948.*

66

The proceedings became definitely hectic and peculiar, so much so that the description of it all defies a rational vocabulary. It called for the cinema, the loudspeaker and Walt Disney at his best.

99

Neville Cardus, *on the joys of Test cricket on a sticky wicket. The days of uncovered pitches are littered with bizarre declarations and remarkable scorecards – including this match where England declared 160 runs behind at 7–68, followed by Australia declaring at 7–32 a mere 15 overs later as both teams sought to get the best of favourable conditions during the first Test at the "Gabba" in 1950–51.*

Pressure, I'll tell you what pressure is… Pressure is a Messerschmitt up your arse. Playing cricket is not.

Keith Miller to Michael Parkinson when asked how he handled pressure. Miller was a RAAF pilot during World War Two before making his test debut as a swashbuckling all-rounder.

66

Greg Chappell at first slip wearing the long-sleeved jumper, wide-brim hat and long-sleeved T-shirt; Ian Chappell at second slip wearing a short-sleeved jumper and wide-brim hat; and Redpath at third slip wearing no jumper at all. Sort of like a progressive striptease!

99

John Arlott, on the fashion choices of the Australian cordon.

We've got a freaker! We've got a
freaker down the wicket now. Not very
shapely and it's masculine. And I would
think it's seen the last of its cricket for
the day. The police are mustered, so are
the cameramen, and Greg Chappell.
And now he's being embraced by a
blond policeman. And this may be
his last public appearance but what a
splendid one.

John Arlott, *commentating on* Test Match Special,
*and failing to remember the word "streaker" at Lord's on
4 August 1975.*

66

Jeez, Henry, she hasn't got bad legs
for an old Sheila, has she?

99

Rodney Hogg *forgets his etiquette lessons during
the Queen's visit to Lord's in 1981.*

After Lillee and Alderman bowled about 15 overs, Kim Hughes said this was it. I did all the stretches and limbering up for the cameras. I waved to my mum in Australia.

Mike Whitney, *at 22 years old, made his Test debut in the last Test of the famous 1981 series after just seven first-class matches. Whitney was playing club cricket in England when he got called up to the XI after Australia's bowling stocks were decimated by injury.*

❝

England have only three major problems. They can't bat, they can't bowl and they can't field.

❞

Martin Johnson, *writing in the* Independent *at the start of the 1986–87 tour, assesses England's chances… After England's recovery to win the Ashes, Johnson later remarked, "Right quote, wrong team."*

A female spectator set up an ironing board and attended to her laundry throughout the fifth day's play.

The Wisden Book of Test Cricket *was less than impressed by Australia's glacial innings, despite perfect conditions for batting. David Boon and Allan Border each took over five hours to make 103 and 100 respectively, at the third Test at the Adelaide Oval, 1987.*

Ladies and gentlemen, welcome to London where it is six degrees outside. I want to wish the Australian team all the best. I know they'll do very well because David Boon has just broken the record, 52 cans [of beer] from Sydney to London.

The pilot of the Qantas flight ferrying the 1989 Ashes touring party acknowledges one of Australian cricket's great off-field records. The original mark was 45 cans of beer set by Rod Marsh in 1983.

What is the world going to think? That Australia has become a namby-pamby nation which doesn't know how to drink? For God's sake, in my day 58 beers between Sydney and London would virtually have classified you as a teetotaller.

Ian Chappell, *unimpressed by the meagre amount of beer consumed. Also unimpressed by David Boon's feat, and the team's behaviour, was the coach, Bob Simpson.*

"

If it had been a cheese roll, it would never have got past him.

"

Graham Gooch, *commenting after Mike Gatting was bowled by Shane Warne's "ball of the century" on Day 2 of the first Test at Old Trafford, 4 June 1993.*

THE BARMY ARMY

Emerging out of the 1994–95 Ashes tour, a group of 30 or so "backpacking" England supporters got together to live out their dream of watching the Ashes Down Under.

Named as such by the Australian media for, reportedly, their hopeless audacity in travelling all the way to Australia in the almost inevitable knowledge that their team would lose, the Barmy Army now has a presence at every international match England plays.

"

English cricket is an irrelevance on and off the ground. And that is not the ramblings of an Anglophobe. It is a statement of fact.

"

Mike Coward, *the Australian journalist, on the English team in the midst of their 1990s doldrums, Australia in England, 1997.*

Somebody told the electronic scoreboard operator about the 500 to 1 odds. He decided to put it up – to give everyone a laugh, I suppose, a bit of black humour.

David Ryder, *the Yorkshire County Cricket Club secretary, recalls the day England defied the odds – literally – in the 1981 Ashes Test at Headingley, coming in at 500 to 1! As reported in* The Guardian, *12 August 2001.*

66

It's very much a game of chess – white-flannelled figures on green grass. 99

Henry Blofeld, *another idiosyncratic description of superfluous detail on Day 4 of the fourth Test at Trent Bridge, 27 August 2005.*

"

Freddie Flintoff is swaying and staggering as he comes on to the top deck of the England team bus. It's been a long night for him.

"

Jonathan Agnew, *commentating on the state of the England team during their parade through London, live on BBC Radio 5 Live, 13 September 2005.*

66

At its best, cricket is the most wonderful entertainment in the world. Vaughan has been a wonderful leader, quietly inspirational and shrewd. To be the best, England must beat the Aussies in Australia, but let's rejoice in the moment. It was a reminder of how good sport can be.

99

Michael Parkinson, *the chat-show host and cricket-loving fan, nails the moment, September 2005.*

Freddie Flintoff's eyes are barely open and his tie is similarly barely held together. He has clearly been sampling the best that No.10 Downing Street has to offer.

Jonathan Agnew, *commenting at the England team's reception with Prime Minister Tony Blair, 13 September 2005.*

66

No foreplay, little titillation. Just wham, bam, thank you ma'am. And not even time for a post-coital cigarette.

99

Charles Happell, Australian journalist, on the cramped schedule for the 2006–07 series. A far cry from the days when a tour went all summer and touring teams played nigh on 40 matches. England in Australia, 2006–07.

He who looks at the clouds takes his eyes off the plough.

Graeme Swann, *urging England to not rely on the weather or good luck to beat the Aussies – as had happened a few times in 2009 and 2010.*

66

They'd win the first four Tests and we'd try to nick one at the end when they were all drunk.

99

Nasser Hussain, *commenting before the start of the 2013 Ashes series. England would go on to win 3–0, July 2013.*

Many times I have cursed the rain in Manchester, but today I would take it home to meet my grandma and marry it.

Graham Swann, *after rain at Old Trafford secured England an unlikely draw on the third Test, thus retaining the Ashes, on 5 August 2013.*

"

We finished third in a two-horse race.

"

Matt Prior, *England's wicketkeeper, summing up England's performance after their 5–0 Ashes thrashing in the 2013–14 tour of Australia.*

We're receiving reports of Aussies in trouble.

Posted on the Nottinghamshire Police Official Twitter account, a tongue-in-cheek tweet as Australia fell to 21 for 5 at Trent Bridge during the fourth Test, 6 August 2015.

"

Stokesy has this finger that we call 'The Claw'. He badly broke it when he was younger and it is almost double the thickness of a normal finger. I genuinely think it helps the ball stick in his hand.

"

Stuart Broad, *commenting on Sky Watchalong's rerun of the 2015 Trent Bridge as Ben Stokes takes a stunning catch to remove Adam Voges.*

Well I'm very flattered, Joe, that you likened me to Albert Einstein – quite a good impression of the late Brian Clough, I thought. But, young man, when your little purple patch comes to an end… I'll have you back in the dock!

Bob Willis delivers a light-hearted response to Joe Root's impersonation of him following England's Ashes win, December 2015.

66

English players only use their feet for *Strictly Come Dancing.*

99

Jarrod Kimber, *on England's shortcomings against spin.*

66 It's worth watching this. How he gets this on. You've got to know how to put one of these rubbers on. There we go. Right to the bottom. Now you put it on, right on the end. And roll it down, right to the bottom. Now pull it right back up…

That's the one. Come on, keep going. And now you've got to knock it down. Push it down, push it down. Pull it down, rub it up. Give it a good rub…

Now you should have a bit of tape round the bottom… keep it in position. **99**

David "Bumble" Lloyd *and his unforgettably hilarious commentary as an Aussie backroom staff member replaced the grip on a bat during the fourth Test at Old Trafford, September 2019.*

66

Aussies are big and empty, just like their country.

99

Ian Botham, *never one to keep his thoughts to himself! As seen on HoldingWilley.com, Haresh Pandya, date unknown.*

When we spoke of literary figures, we spoke of Englishmen. But when we spoke of cricket, we spoke of our own… No Australian had written *Paradise Lost*, but Bradman had made 100 before lunch at Lord's.

Thomas Keneally, *on the pride felt for Australia's cricketers. Though "the Don" made his century before lunch at Leeds, not Lord's.*